O'Dowd

by Iain Gray

Lang Syne

PUBLISHING

WRITING *to* REMEMBER

Lang**Syne**

PUBLISHING

WRITING *to* REMEMBER

Office 5, Vineyard Business Centre,
Pathhead, Midlothian EH37 5XP
Tel: 01875 321 203 Fax: 01875 321 233
E-mail: info@lang-syne.co.uk
www.langsyneshop.co.uk

Design by Dorothy Meikle
Printed by Hay Nisbet Press, Glasgow
© Lang Syne Publishers Ltd 2009

ISBN 978-1-85217-335-7

O'Dowd

MOTTO:
Bravery is best sustained by arms.

CREST:
A hand in armour holding a spear.

NAME variations include:
Ó Dubhda (*Gaelic*)
O'Dowda
Doody
Dowd
Dowds
Duddy

Chapter one:
Origins of Irish surnames

According to an old saying, there are two types of Irish – those who actually are Irish and those who wish they were.

This sentiment is only one example of the allure that the high romance and drama of the proud nation's history holds for thousands of people scattered across the world today.

It's a sad fact, however, that the vast majority of Irish surnames are found far beyond Irish shores, rather than on the Emerald Isle itself.

The population stood at around eight million souls in 1841, but today it stands at fewer than six million.

This is mainly a tragic consequence of the potato famine, also known as the Great Hunger, which devastated Ireland between 1845 and 1849.

The Irish peasantry had become almost wholly reliant for basic sustenance on the potato, first introduced from the Americas in the seventeenth century.

When the crop was hit by a blight, at least 800,000 people starved to death while an estimated two million others were forced to seek a new life far from their native shores – particularly in America, Canada, and Australia.

The effects of the potato blight continued until about 1851, by which time a firm pattern of emigration had become established.

Ireland's loss, however, was to the gain of the countries in which the immigrants settled, contributing enormously, as their descendants do today, to the well being of the nations in which their forefathers settled.

But those who were forced through dire circumstance to establish a new life in foreign parts never forgot their roots, or the proud heritage and traditions of the land that gave them birth.

Nor do their descendants.

It is a heritage that is inextricably bound up in the colourful variety of Irish names themselves – and the origin and history of these names forms an integral part of the vibrant drama that is the nation's history, one of both glorious fortune and tragic misfortune.

This history is well documented, and one of the most important and fascinating of the earliest sources are *The Annals of the Four Masters*, compiled between 1632 and 1636 by four friars at the Franciscan Monastery in County Donegal.

Compiled from earlier sources, and purporting to go back to the Biblical Deluge, much of the material takes in the mythological origins and history of Ireland and the Irish.

This includes tales of successive waves of invaders and settlers such as the Fomorians, the Partholonians, the Nemedians, the Fir Bolgs, the Tuatha De Danann, and the Laigain.

Of particular interest are the *Milesian Genealogies*

because the majority of Irish clans today claim a descent from either Heremon, Ir, or Heber – three of the sons of Milesius, a king of what is now modern day Spain.

These sons invaded Ireland in the second millennium B.C, apparently in fulfilment of a mysterious prophecy received by their father.

This Milesian lineage is said to have ruled Ireland for nearly 3,000 years, until the island came under the sway of England's King Henry II in 1171 following what is known as the Cambro-Norman invasion.

This is an important date not only in Irish history in general, but for the effect the invasion subsequently had for Irish surnames.

'Cambro' comes from the Welsh, and 'Cambro-Norman' describes those Welsh knights of Norman origin who invaded Ireland.

But they were invaders who stayed, inter-marrying with the native Irish population and founding their own proud dynasties that bore Cambro-Norman names such as Archer, Barbour, Brannagh, Fitzgerald, Fitzgibbon, Fleming, Joyce, Plunkett, and Walsh – to name only a few.

These 'Cambro-Norman' surnames that still flourish throughout the world today form one of the three main categories in which Irish names can be placed – those of Gaelic-Irish, Cambro-Norman, and Anglo-Irish.

Previous to the Cambro-Norman invasion of the twelfth century, and throughout the earlier invasions and settlement of those wild bands of sea rovers known as the Vikings in the eighth and ninth centuries, the population of the island was relatively small, and it was normal for a person to be identified through the use of only a forename.

But as population gradually increased and there were many more people with the same forename, surnames were adopted to distinguish one person, or one community, from another.

Individuals identified themselves with their own particular tribe, or 'tuath', and this tribe – that also became known as a clann, or clan – took its name from some distinguished ancestor who had founded the clan.

The Gaelic-Irish form of the name Kelly, for example, is Ó Ceallaigh, or O'Kelly, indicating descent from an original 'Ceallaigh', with the 'O' denoting 'grandson of.' The name was later anglicised to Kelly.

The prefix 'Mac' or 'Mc', meanwhile, as with the clans of the Scottish Highlands, denotes 'son of.'

Although the Irish clans had much in common with their Scottish counterparts, one important difference lies in what are known as 'septs', or branches, of the clan.

Septs of Scottish clans were groups who often bore an entirely different name from the clan name but were under the clan's protection.

In Ireland, septs were groups that shared the same name and who could be found scattered throughout the four provinces of Ulster, Leinster, Munster, and Connacht.

The 'golden age' of the Gaelic-Irish clans, infused as their veins were with the blood of Celts, pre-dates the Viking invasions of the eighth and ninth centuries and the Norman invasion of the twelfth century, and the sacred heart of the country was the Hill of Tara, near the River Boyne, in County Meath.

Known in Gaelic as 'Teamhar na Rí', or Hill of Kings, it was the royal seat of the 'Ard Rí Éireann', or High King of Ireland, to whom the petty kings, or chieftains, from the island's provinces were ultimately subordinate.

It was on the Hill of Tara, beside a stone pillar known as the Irish 'Lia Fáil', or Stone of Destiny, that the High Kings were inaugurated and, according to legend, this stone would emit a piercing screech that could be heard all over Ireland when touched by the hand of the rightful king.

The Hill of Tara is today one of the island's main tourist attractions.

Opposition to English rule over Ireland, established in the wake of the Cambro-Norman invasion, broke out frequently and the harsh solution adopted by the powerful forces of the Crown was to forcibly evict the native Irish from their lands.

These lands were then granted to Protestant colonists, or 'planters', from Britain.

Many of these colonists, ironically, came from Scotland and were the descendants of the original 'Scotti', or 'Scots', who gave their name to Scotland after migrating there in the fifth century A.D., from the north of Ireland.

Colonisation entailed harsh penal laws being imposed on the majority of the native Irish population, stripping them practically of all of their rights.

The Crown's main bastion in Ireland was Dublin and its environs, known as the Pale, and it was the dispossessed peasantry who lived outside this Pale, desperately striving to eke out a meagre living.

It was this that gave rise to the modern-day expression of someone or something being 'beyond the pale'.

Attempts were made to stamp out all aspects of the ancient Gaelic-Irish culture, to the extent that even to bear a Gaelic-Irish name was to invite discrimination.

This is why many Gaelic-Irish names were anglicised with, for example, and noted above, Ó Ceallaigh, or O'Kelly, being anglicised to Kelly.

Succeeding centuries have seen strong revivals of Gaelic-Irish consciousness, however, and this has led to many families reverting back to the original form of their name, while the language itself is frequently found on the fluent tongues of an estimated 90,000 to 145,000 of the island's population.

Ireland's turbulent history of religious and political strife is one that lasted well into the twentieth century, a landmark century that saw the partition of the island into the twenty-six counties of the independent Republic of

Ireland, or Eire, and the six counties of Northern Ireland, or Ulster.

Dublin, originally founded by Vikings, is now a vibrant and truly cosmopolitan city while the proud city of Belfast is one of the jewels in the crown of Ulster.

It was Saint Patrick who first brought the light of Christianity to Ireland in the fifth century A.D.

Interpretations of this Christian message have varied over the centuries, often leading to bitter sectarian conflict – but the many intricately sculpted Celtic Crosses found all over the island are symbolic of a unity that crosses the sectarian divide.

It is an image that fuses the 'old gods' of the Celts with Christianity.

All the signs from the early years of this new millennium indicate that sectarian strife may soon become a thing of the past – with the Irish and their many kinsfolk across the world, be they Protestant or Catholic, finding common purpose in the rich tapestry of their shared heritage.

Chapter two:
Royal lineage

The modern day counties of Sligo and Mayo, in the ancient western province of Connacht, were for centuries home on the Emerald Isle to bearers of the name of O'Dowd.

The Gaelic form of the name is Ó Dubhda, stemming from 'dubh', meaning 'black', and it was in the baronies of Tireragh in Sligo and those of Tirawley and Erris in Mayo that the original Ó Dubhdas flourished.

A separate sept was also to be found in modern day Co. Derry, in the northern province of Ulster, where the name survives to this day in the more commonly found form of Duddy.

Of truly royal pedigree, the O'Dowds of Connacht were the principal clan of the tribal grouping known as the Uí Fiachrach, a confederation that included equally proud clans such as the Houlihans, Shaughnessys, Quigleys, Finnegans and O'Clearys.

'Ui Fíachrach' indicates a direct line of descent from one of Ireland's greatest warrior kings – none other than Niall Noíghiallach, better known to posterity as Niall of the Nine Hostages, through his brother Fiachra.

The dramatic life and times of this illustrious ancestor of the O'Dowds are steeped in stirring Celtic myth and legend.

The youngest son of Eochaidh Mugmedon, king of the province of Connacht, his mother died in childbirth and he was brought up by his evil stepmother Mongfhinn who was determined that he should die. She accordingly abandoned him naked on the Hill of Tara, inauguration site of the Ard Rí, or High Kings of Ireland, but a wandering bard found him and took him back to his father.

One legend is that Mongfhinn sent Niall and his four brothers – Brian, Fiachra, Ailill and Fergus – to a renowned prophet who was also a blacksmith to determine which of them would succeed their father as Ard Rí.

The blacksmith, known as Sitchin, set the lads a task by deliberately setting fire to his forge.

Niall's brothers ran in and came out carrying the spearheads, fuel, hammers, and barrels of beer that they had rescued, but Niall staggered out clutching the heavy anvil so vital to the blacksmith's trade.

By this deed, Sitchin prophesied that Niall would be the one who would take on the glorious mantle of kingship.

Another prophetic incident occurred one day while Niall and his brothers were engaged in the hunt.

Thirsty from their efforts they encountered an ugly old woman who offered them water – but only in return for a kiss.

Three of the lads, no doubt repelled by her green teeth and scaly skin, refused. Fiachra pecked her lightly on the cheek and, by this act, she prophesied that he would one day reign at Tara – but only briefly.

The bold Niall, however, kissed her fully on the lips. The hag then demanded that he should now have full sexual intercourse with her and, undaunted, he did so.

Through this action she was suddenly transformed into a stunningly beautiful young woman known as Flaithius, or Royalty, who predicted that he would become the greatest High King of Ireland.

His stepmother Mongfhinn later tried to poison him, but accidentally took the deadly potion herself and died.

This legend relates to what was known as the Festival of Mongfhinn, or Feis na Samhan (the Feast of Samhain), because it was on the evening of October 31, on Samhain's Eve, that the poisoning incident is said to have taken place.

It was believed for centuries in Ireland that, on Samhain Eve, Mongfhinn's warped and wicked spirit would roam the land in hungry search of children's souls.

The Festival, or Feast, of Samhain, is today better known as Hallowe'en.

Niall became Ard Rí in 379 A.D. and embarked on the series of military campaigns and other daring adventures that would subsequently earn him the title of Niall of the Nine Hostages. The nine countries and territories into which he raided and took hostages for ransom were the Irish provinces of Munster, Leinster, Connacht, and Ulster, Britain, and the territories of the Saxons, Morini, Picts and Dalriads.

Niall's most famous hostage was a young lad known as Succat, son of Calpernius, a Romano-Briton who lived in the area of present day Milford Haven, on the Welsh coast.

Later known as Patricius, or Patrick, he became renowned as Ireland's patron saint, St. Patrick, responsible for bringing the light of Christianity to the island in the early years of the fifth century A.D.

Raiding in Gaul, in the area of Boulogne-sur-mer in present day France, Niall was ambushed and killed by one of his treacherous subjects in 405 A.D.

But his legacy survived through the royal dynasties and clans founded by his sons and brothers such as Fiachra.

It is also through Fiachra that the O'Dowds can trace a descent from Daithi, the last pagan king of Ireland.

Daithi was certainly well travelled – because he was killed after being struck by a bolt of lightning while leading a Celtic army to the foothills of the Alps in about 455 A.D.

Ruling as Princes of Uí Fiachrach, the inauguration site of the O'Dowd chieftains was at Carn Amhalghaigh, near Killala, and one of the treasured possessions of the Republic of Ireland's National Museum in Dublin is a manuscript account of the inauguration ceremony.

Known as the *Great Book of Lecan*, it is thought to have been compiled between the late fourteenth and early fifteenth centuries.

The O'Dowds protected their territory with no less than 20 castles, and the forlorn ruins of one of them, Rathlee, can be seen to this day near the harbour of the village of Rathlee in Co. Sligo.

These castles were to stand them in good stead, unfortunately only for a time, in the wake of the devastating Norman invasion of the island in the late twelfth century and the subsequent consolidation of the power of the English Crown.

English dominion over Ireland was ratified through the Treaty of Windsor of 1175, under the terms of which native Irish clan chieftains were only allowed to rule territory unoccupied by the Anglo-Normans in the role of a vassal of the English monarch.

Further waves of ambitious and land-hungry Anglo-Norman adventurers arrived in droves over the succeeding decades, but the O'Dowds of Connacht, in common with their native Irish counterparts in Ulster, proved particularly resilient in resisting their encroachment on their territories.

In 1354, for example, Sen-Bhrain O'Dowd managed to oust Anglo-Normans who had managed to gain a foothold in Tireragh.

But, increasingly, the native Irish found themselves fighting a rearguard action and their only recourse was organised rebellion.

No one was immune from vicious reprisal every time rebellion broke out and was quashed, and among the many victims was Father John O'Dowd, a Franciscan, who in 1579 was brutally tortured before being summarily hanged.

Chapter three:

Victory and defeat

The plight of the O'Dowds and other Irish clans only went from bad to worse over a policy known as 'plantation', or settlement of loyal Protestants on lands previously held by the Gaelic-Irish.

This policy had started during the reign from 1491 to 1547 of Henry VIII, whose Reformation effectively outlawed the established Roman Catholic faith throughout his dominions.

This plantation continued throughout the subsequent reigns of Elizabeth I, James I (James VI of Scotland), Charles I, and in the aftermath of the Cromwellian invasion of the island in 1649.

Rebellion erupted in 1594, and at its forefront was the O'Donnell chieftain Aodh Rua Ó Domhmaill, better known as Red Hugh O'Donnell.

In what became known as the *Cogadh na Naoi mBliama*, or the Nine Years War, Red Hugh and his allies who included the O'Dowds and the Gallaghers, literally set the island ablaze in a vicious campaign of guerrilla warfare.

It was under Red Hugh that they wreaked a whirlwind of devastation on English settlements and garrisons in a daring series of lightning raids.

In 1596, allied with the forces of Hugh O'Neill, Earl of Tyrone, Red Hugh and his allies inflicted a defeat on an English army at the battle of Clontibert, while in August of 1598 another significant defeat was inflicted at the battle of Yellow Ford.

But the most significant defeat inflicted on the English forces during the Nine Years War came at the battle of Curlew Pass, fought on the hot summer day of August 15th, 1599, near Boyle, Co. Roscommon, in the northwest of the island.

With O'Dowds in their ranks, the rebels ambushed an English force under the command of Sir Conyers Clifford at a pass through the imposing Curlew Mountains and routed them.

The English lost at least 500 men, including Sir Conyers Clifford, whose head was cut off and triumphantly given to Red Hugh.

The Curlew Pass was the scene of another rebel victory later in the war, while the battlefield today is overlooked by a magnificent sculpture, the Gaelic Chieftain, which was executed by the sculptor Maurice Harron and placed there in 1999.

As English control over Ireland teetered on the brink of collapse, thousands more troops, including mercenaries, were hastily despatched to the island and, in the face of the overwhelming odds against them, Red Hugh and the Earl of Tyrone sought help from England's enemy, Spain.

A well-equipped Spanish army under General del Áquila landed at Kinsale in December of 1601, but was forced to surrender only a few weeks later, in January of 1602.

Resistance continued until 1603, but proved abortive.

Despite vicious reprisals by the authorities and the confiscation of vast swathes of land, it took less than forty years for another rebellion to devastate the island – one fuelled primarily by the policy of plantation.

In the insurrection that exploded in 1641, at least 2,000 Protestant settlers were massacred, while thousands more were stripped of their belongings and driven from their lands.

England had its own distractions with the Civil War that culminated in the execution of Charles I in 1649, and from 1641 to 1649 Ireland was ruled by a rebel group known as the Irish Catholic Confederation, or the Confederation of Kilkenny – and O'Dowds were prominent among them.

Terrible as the atrocities against the Protestant settlers had been, subsequent accounts became greatly exaggerated, serving to fuel a burning desire for revenge.

Following the execution of Charles I and the consolidation of the power of England's Oliver Cromwell, the time was ripe for vengeance in a terrible form.

Cromwell descended on Ireland at the head of a 20,000-strong army that landed at Ringford, near Dublin, in August of 1649.

He had three main aims: to quash all forms of rebellion, to 'remove' all Catholic landowners who had taken part in the rebellion and to convert the native Irish to the Protestant faith.

An early warning of the terrors that were in store came when the northeastern town of Drogheda was stormed and taken in September and between 2,000 and 4,000 of its inhabitants killed.

The defenders of Drogheda's St. Peter's Church, who had refused to surrender, were burned to death as they huddled for refuge in the steeple and the church was deliberately torched.

A similar fate befell Wexford, on the southeast coast, where at least 1,500 of its inhabitants were slaughtered, including 200 defenceless women, despite their pathetic pleas for mercy.

Three hundred other inhabitants of the town drowned when their overladen boats sank as they desperately tried to flee to safety, while a group of Franciscan friars were massacred in their church – some as they knelt before the altar.

The Wexford massacre is commemorated today in the form of a statue and plaque at the town's Bull Ring.

Cromwell soon held the land in a grip of iron, allowing him to implement what amounted to a policy of ethnic cleansing.

His troopers were given free rein to hunt down and kill

priests, while rebel estates were confiscated, including those of the O'Dowds.

An estimated 11 million acres of land were confiscated, and an edict was issued stating that any native Irish found east of the River Shannon after May 1, 1654, faced either summary execution or transportation to the West Indies.

Later in the seventeenth century, the island was devastated yet again in what was known as *Cogadh an Dá Rí*, or the War of the Two Kings.

Also known as the Williamite War or the Jacobite War in Ireland, it was sparked off in 1688 when the Stuart monarch James II (James VII of Scotland) was deposed and fled into French exile.

The Protestant William of Orange and his wife Mary were invited to take up the thrones of Scotland, Ireland, and England – but James still had significant support in Ireland, with his supporters known as Jacobites.

Following the arrival in England of William and Mary from Holland, Richard Talbot, 1st Earl of Tyrconnell and James's Lord Deputy in Ireland, assembled an army loyal to the Stuart cause, and among them were the O'Dowds.

The aim was to garrison and fortify the island in the name of James and quell any resistance.

Londonderry, or Derry, proved loyal to the cause of William of Orange, or William III as he had become, and managed to hold out against a siege that was not lifted until July 28, 1689.

James, with the support of troops and money supplied by Louis XIV of France, had landed at Kinsale in March of 1689 and joined forces with his Irish supporters.

A series of military encounters followed, culminating in James's defeat by an army commanded by William at the battle of the Boyne on July 12, 1690.

Among the many Jacobite dead was an O'Dowd officer who was reputed to have been 7ft. tall.

There may well be some truth in this – because to this day a significant number of bearers of the O'Dowd name are noted for their well above- average height.

James, meanwhile, fled again into French exile, never to return, while another significant Jacobite defeat occurred in July of 1691 at the battle of Aughrim – with about half their army killed on the field, wounded or taken prisoner.

The Williamite forces besieged Limerick and the Jacobites were forced into surrender in September of 1691.

A peace treaty, known as the Treaty of Limerick followed, under which those Jacobites willing to swear an oath of loyalty to William were allowed to remain in their native land.

Those reluctant to do so were allowed to seek exile in foreign lands – but their ancient homelands were lost to them forever.

A further flight overseas occurred following an abortive rebellion in 1798, while O'Dowds were among the many thousands of Irish who were forced to seek a new life many thousands of miles from their native land during the famine known as The Great Hunger, caused by a failure of the potato crop between 1845 and 1849.

But in many cases Ireland's loss of sons and daughters such as the O'Dowds was to the gain of those nations in which they forged new lives for themselves.

Chapter four:

On the world stage

From music and sport to art and politics, bearers of the O'Dowd name, in all the variations of spelling of the surname, have stamped their mark at an international level.

Born in 1961 in London of Irish parentage, George Alan O'Dowd is the singer and songwriter better known as **Boy George**.

Frequently in the newspaper headlines for his antics off stage, he was one of the leading lights of what was known as the English 'New Romantic' movement of the early 1980s.

This was as the singer with the band Culture Club, whose debut album was the 1982 *Kissing to be Clever* and whose most memorable hit singles include *Karma Chameleon* and *Do You Really Want to Hurt Me*?

Boy George caused a sensation when he first hit the music scene because of his rather exotic androgynous appearance, while he later became the subject of controversy over what was then his drug addiction and his arrests for a number of misdemeanours.

Culture Club disbanded in 1986, and while Boy George continued to enjoy a successful solo career, in August of 2006 a judge sentenced him to community service for falsely reporting a burglary in his Manhattan apartment.

This involved him having to spend a period picking up garbage for the New York City Department of Sanitation, an event recorded by the world's media.

In addition to his solo recording career, Boy George now also enjoys a reputation as a disc jockey on the club scene.

In a different musical genre and leading a decidedly less controversial lifestyle, **Seamus O'Dowd**, also known as Seamie O'Dowd, is the Irish musician who was born in Maugheraboy, Co. Sligo.

An accomplished performer on a range of instruments that include mandolin, guitar and fiddle and a former member of the Irish band Dervish, he is the son of the noted traditional Irish musicians **Sheila** and **Joel O'Dowd**.

Behind the music stage **Tom Dowd** was the pioneering recording engineer and record producer who was born in 1925 in Manhattan.

With his mother an opera singer and his father a concertmaster, it is perhaps not surprising that Dowd's first love was music.

He grew up learning to play the string bass, tuba, piano and violin but, excelling in the sciences at school, his first employment was as a physicist at Columbia University.

Drafted into the army in 1943, his scientific background led to him being co-opted to serve in the Manhattan Project

– the vast and secret enterprise that led to the development during the Second World War of the atomic bomb.

Returning to his passion for music at the end of the war, he was employed as a recording engineer with Atlantic Records, recording popular artists who included Ray Charles, The Coasters, Bobby Darin and The Drifters.

Pioneering the use of the multi-track recording method and popularising the use of stereo sound, his recording expertise was later in high demand from solo artists and bands that included Aretha Franklin, Booker T. and the MGs, Eric Clapton, Lynyrd Skynyrd, Chicago, Cream and Dusty Springfield.

He died in 2002, only a few months after receiving a Grammy Trustees Award for his lifetime achievement in music, while *Tom Dowd and the Language of Music*, an award-winning documentary about his life, was screened a year later.

In the highly competitive world of sport **Craig Dowd**, born in 1969 in Auckland, is the former New Zealand rugby union player who was a member of his national team from 1993 to 2000.

Other teams he played for include the Auckland Suburbs, Auckland, and Auckland Blues, while he has also coached English team the London Wasps.

On the golf course Dakoda Flowie Dowd, better known as **Koda Dowd,** is the American amateur golfer who was born in 1993.

It was in April of 2006, only a few days after her 13th birthday that she became the youngest player ever to compete in the Ladies Professional Golf Association Tournament.

Nicknamed 'The St. Paul Cyclone', **Mike O'Dowd** was the champion boxer born in 1895 in St. Paul, Minnesota, who died in 1957.

Middleweight boxing champion of the world from 1917 to 1920, he was the only champion to fight at the front during the First World War, serving in the U.S. Army.

The first woman to perform the arduous feats of reaching the summit of Mount Everest from the forbidding peak's north and south sides, **Cathy O'Dowd** is the South African climber, mountaineer and author who was born in 1969 in Johannesburg.

O'Dowd, who is married to fellow South African mountaineer Ian Woodall, managed to reach the summit of Everest from its south side in 1996, following the feat three years later by successfully tackling the north side.

Her books include the 2001 *Just for the love of it* and, with her husband, the 1998 *Everest: Free to Decide*.

In the world of books **Annie O'Dowd**, born in 1962 in Brisbane, is the Australian author and illustrator of the highly popular *Seadog Adventures* series of books for children, while in the world of journalism **Maureen Dowd**, born in 1952, is the noted American newspaper columnist based in Washington D.C. for the *New York Times*.

Awarded a prestigious Pulitzer Prize in 1999 for her series of columns on the scandal involving U.S. President Bill Clinton and his aide Monica Lewinsky, she is also a recipient of a Matrix Award from New York Women in Communications.

Born in 1953 in Thurles, Co. Tipperary, **Niall O'Dowd** is a prominent Irish-American author and journalist.

Immigrating to the United States in 1979, he not only later founded a number of publications that include the *Irish America* magazine, but also acted as an intermediary during President Clinton's administration between the White House and Ireland's Sinn Féin political party – leading up to what became known as the Good Friday peace agreement.

He is a younger brother of the Republic of Ireland Fine Gael Party politician **Fergus O'Dowd** who, at the time of writing, is his party's spokesman for Transport and Marine.

Also in the world of politics and political activism **Douglas Dowd**, born in 1919, is the American political economist, historian and critic of capitalism whose books include the 1997 *Blues for America: A Critique, A Lament, and Some Memories.*

Born in 1949, **Jeff Dowd** is the American political activist and television producer who is best known as one of the group called 'the Seattle Seven' who were briefly imprisoned for contempt of court for their part in protests against the Vietnam War.

Later establishing himself as an independent film producer and promoter, he acted as co-executive producer for the 1992 *FernGully: The Last Rainforest*, and as executive producer for the 2002 television movie *The Last Game*.

The son of Irish immigrants to Australia **Bernard O'Dowd**, born in 1866 in Victoria, showed early promise when, aged only eight, he was able to read poet John Milton's *Paradise Lost*.

His love of the written word led to him becoming not only an assistant librarian for the Supreme Court at Melbourne, but also a chief Parliamentary draughtsman.

His socialist principals led to his co-founding the radical newspaper *Tocsin*, while his poetic works include the 1903 *Downward* and the 1921 *Alma Venus*.

The words from one of his poems are inscribed around the Federation Pavilion in Sydney's Centennial Park – designed 35 years after O'Dowd's death in 1953.

In the world of acting **Chris O'Dowd**, born in 1980 in Boyle, Co. Roscommon, is the Irish actor who won a 2005 Scottish BAFTA award for his role in the film *Festival*.

The popular actor has also starred in the British television comedy *The IT Crowd* and the docu-drama *The Year London Blew Up*.

On an artistic note, Robert Dowd was the American artist born in 1936 in Grand Rapids, Michigan, and who painted under the name of **Robert O'Dowd**.

It was following his discharge from the U.S. Marines in 1957 that he found his true vocation in art.

He began by painting everyday objects such as traffic signs, an art technique that culminated in a famous exhibition at the Pasadena Art Museum in 1962 featuring the work of artists who included O'Dowd and Andy Warhol.

Their style and technique became known as 'Pop Art', and we also have O'Dowd to thank for that everyday kitchen item, the fridge magnet.

The artist, who died in 1996, started the fridge magnet craze by fashioning miniature chocolate chip cookies with magnets attached to their backs.

Key dates in Ireland's history from the first settlers to the formation of the Irish Republic:

circa 7000 B.C.	Arrival and settlement of Stone Age people.
circa 3000 B.C.	Arrival of settlers of New Stone Age period.
circa 600 B.C.	First arrival of the Celts.
200 A.D.	Establishment of Hill of Tara, Co. Meath, as seat of the High Kings.
circa 432 A.D.	Christian mission of St. Patrick.
800-920 A.D.	Invasion and subsequent settlement of Vikings.
1002 A.D.	Brian Boru recognised as High King.
1014	Brian Boru killed at battle of Clontarf.
1169-1170	Cambro-Norman invasion of the island.
1171	Henry II claims Ireland for the English Crown.
1366	Statutes of Kilkenny ban marriage between native Irish and English.
1529-1536	England's Henry VIII embarks on religious Reformation.
1536	Earl of Kildare rebels against the Crown.
1541	Henry VIII declared King of Ireland.
1558	Accession to English throne of Elizabeth I.
1565	Battle of Affane.
1569-1573	First Desmond Rebellion.
1579-1583	Second Desmond Rebellion.
1594-1603	Nine Years War.
1606	Plantation' of Scottish and English settlers.
1607	Flight of the Earls.
1632-1636	Annals of the Four Masters compiled.
1641	Rebellion over policy of plantation and other grievances.
1649	Beginning of Cromwellian conquest.
1688	Flight into exile in France of Catholic Stuart monarch James II as Protestant Prince William of Orange invited to take throne of England along with his wife, Mary.
1689	William and Mary enthroned as joint monarchs; siege of Derry.
1690	Jacobite forces of James defeated by William at battle of the Boyne (July) and Dublin taken.

1691	Athlone taken by William; Jacobite defeats follow at Aughrim, Galway, and Limerick; conflict ends with Treaty of Limerick (October) and Irish officers allowed to leave for France.
1695	Penal laws introduced to restrict rights of Catholics; banishment of Catholic clergy.
1704	Laws introduced constricting rights of Catholics in landholding and public office.
1728	Franchise removed from Catholics.
1791	Foundation of United Irishmen republican movement.
1796	French invasion force lands in Bantry Bay.
1798	Defeat of Rising in Wexford and death of United Irishmen leaders Wolfe Tone and Lord Edward Fitzgerald.
1800	Act of Union between England and Ireland.
1803	Dublin Rising under Robert Emmet.
1829	Catholics allowed to sit in Parliament.
1845-1849	The Great Hunger: thousands starve to death as potato crop fails and thousands more emigrate.
1856	Phoenix Society founded.
1858	Irish Republican Brotherhood established.
1873	Foundation of Home Rule League.
1893	Foundation of Gaelic League.
1904	Foundation of Irish Reform Association.
1913	Dublin strikes and lockout.
1916	Easter Rising in Dublin and proclamation of an Irish Republic.
1917	Irish Parliament formed after Sinn Fein election victory.
1919-1921	War between Irish Republican Army and British Army.
1922	Irish Free State founded, while six northern counties remain part of United Kingdom as Northern Ireland or Ulster; civil war up until 1923 between rival republican groups.
1949	Foundation of Irish Republic after all remaining constitutional links with Britain are severed.